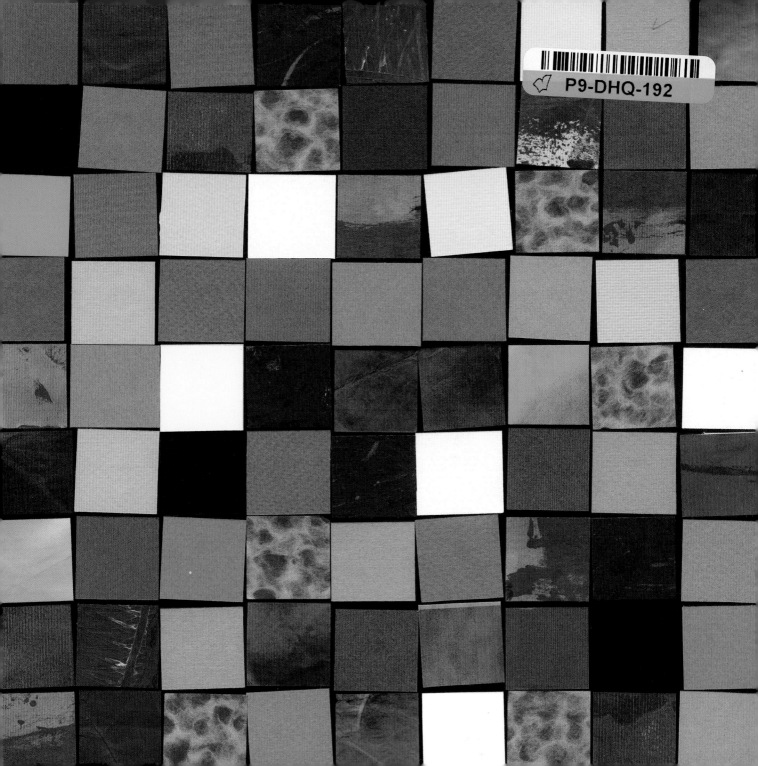

To Alice Brewster, Barbara Bender,
and their kindergartners.

Library of Congress Cataloging-in-Publication Data
Barner, Bob.
Bears! bears! bears! / by Bob Barner.
p. cm.
ISBN 978-0-8118-7057-3 (alk. paper)
1. Bears–Juvenile literature. I. Title.
QL737.C27B3577 2010
599.78–dc22
2009040860

Book design by Amy E. Achaibou.
Typeset in Antique Central and Today SH.
The illustrations in this book were rendered in collage.

Manufactured by Leefung, Da Ling Shan Town, Dongguan, China, in November 2009.

1 3 5 7 9 10 8 6 4 2

This product conforms to CPSIA 2008.

Chronicle Books LLC
680 Second Street, San Francisco, California 94107

www.chroniclekids.com

Bears! Bears! Bears!

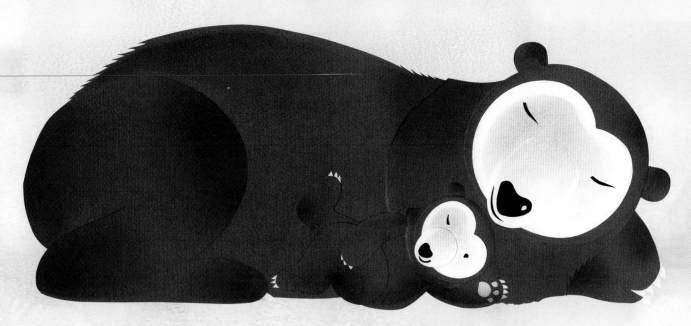

By Bob Barner

chronicle books · san francisco

Bears! Bears! Bears!

I want to see a world of bears.

Polar bears
dive for an
icy seal.

Sun bears lick
up a sticky meal.

Giant pandas munch bamboo
with a snap.

Spectacled bears cuddle up for a nap.

Grizzly bears
fish with
giant claws.

Sloth bears hug mama

with furry paws.

Moon bears climb tall trees with a leap.

Black bears doze in

Bears! Bears! Bears!
I want to see diving, licking,

munching, cuddling, fishing,
hugging, climbing, dozing bears.

Baby Bears!

SUN BEAR

Cubs stay with their mother until adulthood.

SPECTACLED BEAR

Babies' eyes stay closed for the first month.

MOON BEAR

Cubs stay with their mother for two to three years.

GIANT PANDA BEAR

Cubs are born the size of a stick of butter.

GRIZZLY BEAR

Cubs grow up to be 9 feet tall and 1,000 pounds.

BLACK BEAR

Cubs can't walk until they are four to five weeks old.

SLOTH BEAR

Born in a den, cubs won't come outside for several months.

POLAR BEAR

At birth, cubs weigh about 1 pound.

Polar bears live around the Arctic Circle from Canada to Russia.

Sun bears live in the tropical rainforests of Indonesia, Malaysia, and Vietnam.

Giant pandas live in a small area of central China.

Spectacled bears are the only bear species that is native to South America.

NORTH AMERICA

SOUTH AMERICA

the WORLD!

EUROPE

ASIA

AFRICA

AUSTRALIA

ANTARCTICA

Grizzly bears, a type of brown bear, live in Canada and Alaska. Other brown bears live in Europe and Asia.

Brown bears

Sloth bears live in the grasslands and forests of southern Asia, including India and Nepal.

Black bears live in the mountains and woodlands of North America.

Moon bears (Asiatic black bears) are spread across Asia from Pakistan to Japan.